Reading Quaker Meeting

Also published by Two Rivers Press

Reading Poets: A New Anthology edited by Vic Pickup
Reading Gaol: A Short History by Peter Stoneley
The Happy Prince by Oscar Wilde, illustrated by Sally Castle
Coley Talking by Margaret Ounsley
Bricks & Brickwork in Reading: Patterns & Polychromy by Adam Sowan
Reading's Influential Women by Terry Dixon & Linda Saul
The Art and History of Whiteknights edited by Jenny Halstead
Just a Moment by Ian House
The Art of Peter Hay by John Froy with Martin Andrews
Signs of the Times: Reading's Memorials by Malcolm Summers
Rural Reading by Adrian Lawson & Geoff Sawers
Reading Abbey and the Abbey Quarter by Peter Durrant & John Painter
Reading's Bayeux Tapestry by Reading Museum
Picture Palace to Penny Plunge: Reading's Cinemas by David Cliffe
Whispers of Better Things: Green Belts to National Trust: How the Hill Family Changed Our World by Duncan Mackay
Edith Morley Before and After: Reminiscences of a Working Life edited by Barbara Morris
Silchester: Life on the Dig by Jenny Halstead & Michael Fulford
Allen W. Seaby: Art and Nature by Martin Andrews & Robert Gillmor
Fox Talbot & the Reading Establishment by Martin Andrews
All Change at Reading by Adam Sowan
Caversham Court Gardens: A Heritage Guide by Friends of Caversham Court Gardens
Broad Street Chapel and the Origins of Dissent in Reading by Geoff Sawers
Believing in Reading: Our Places of Worship by Adam Sowan
The Arts of Peace: An Anthology of Poetry edited by Adrian Blamires and Peter Robinson
An Artist's Year in the Harris Garden by Jenny Halstead
The Reading Quiz Book by Adam Sowan
A Mark of Affection: The Soane Obelisk in Reading by Adam Sowan
A Thames Bestiary by Peter Hay and Geoff Sawers
Roots and Branches: The Centenary History of Battle and Caversham Libraries, Reading by David Cliffe

Reading Quaker Meeting

A history

First published in the UK in 2024 by Two Rivers Press
7 Denmark Road, Reading RG1 5PA
www.tworiverspress.com

ISBN 978-1-915048-22-6

1 2 3 4 5 6 7 8 9

Two Rivers Press is represented in the UK by Inpress Ltd
and distributed by BookSource, Glasgow.

Cover design by Nadja Robinson with a painting by Geoff Sawers
Text design by Nadja Robinson and typeset in Parisine

Printed and bound in Great Britain by Halstan, Amersham

Contents

Quakers, *or* The Religious Society of Friends

> The humble, meek, merciful, just, pious, and devout souls
> are everywhere of one religion; and when death has taken
> off the mask they will know one another, though the divers
> liveries they wear here makes them strangers.
> — William Penn, 1693

Quakers – also known as The Religious Society of Friends – try to live in truth, peace, simplicity and equality, finding something of God in everyone including ourselves, in community and in the natural world. Quakers have roots in Christianity but value the insights of other faiths as well. Meeting together in worship that begins in silence but is open to anyone to speak enables a diversity of beliefs and voices; as such it is central to Quaker spiritual practice. Quakers in the UK are grouped into many local Meetings; this book outlines the history of Reading Meeting and its place within the town, and of the Meeting House itself.

I. Early days and persecution

Quakers have a long history in Reading, almost from their earliest times.

During the English Civil Wars of the 1640s soldiers in Parliament's New Model Army were encouraged to think independently, be selective over their ministers and even preach themselves; after many years of dissatisfaction with the established Church hierarchy new movements began to emerge from the roots of society. Freedom of the press under the new Commonwealth meant that anyone could publish their ideas.

An isolated congregation in the Westmorland fells began to worship in silence without any leadership or ritual, and in 1652 they met an itinerant shoemaker called George Fox. Together they became the 'Friends of Truth', often just 'Friends', and they soon became known derisively as 'Quakers'; brought up before magistrates on a charge of blasphemy, Fox 'bade them tremble at the word of the Lord', but the name stuck and was happily adopted. Denying dogma and legalism, the Friends would accept only the guidance of the 'inner light' of God, arguing that their consciences told them what was right and lawful regardless of the law of the land. Oliver Cromwell's control of the army depended on him portraying himself as a champion of religious freedom. He is said to have remarked in 1654:

> Now I see there's a people risen, that I cannot win either with Gifts, Honours, Offices or Places; but all other Sects and People, I can.

Members of the Westmorland group were soon travelling around England and Wales on horse or on foot, preaching and holding meetings. Miles Halhead and Thomas Salthouse arrived in the town of Reading early in 1655, holding public meetings at the 'Broad Face Bowling Green' (behind the Market Place), at the Baptist meeting place by the Forbury, and at the house of a wealthy woollen-draper named Thomas Curtis in Sun Lane, near where the George Inn still stands. The second of these meetings was 'much obstructed by reason of ye Opposition & disturbance made by some ill-minded persons' but nevertheless they found a ready audience and many were brought into the group.

George Fox visited Reading a few months later and addressed a 'glorious' open air Reading meeting in 'George Lamboll's orchard' when

> almost all the whole town came together... and a great
> convincement of people there was that day, and people
> were mightily satisfied. And there was a great meeting
> settled there.

Edward Burrough and Francis Howgill from Westmorland too made repeated visits to the town, encouraging and building up the community. This early Quaker meeting may have numbered a hundred or so people, in a town of five to six thousand. Quakers refused to pay the compulsory tithe of 10 per cent of their produce or income to maintain the Church of England and were scornful of the 'hireling priests', asserting that inspiration to preach could come from anyone. The established Church was seen simply to support the interests of power and wealth, and Quakers frequently described church tithes as 'the mark of the Beast'.

In 1655 Leonard Cole 'suffer'd Imprisonment in Reading Goal [sic] about six Weeks, and soon after his Discharge had taken from him, for five Shillings demanded for Tithe, an Horse worth four Pounds.' We only know this from Quaker sources; the official court records from this time are patchy or lost, but a Quaker tradition of clear record-keeping is helpful when we come to try to write history. The next year we find that

> Joseph Cole, Dorothy Waugh, George Adamson, Hannah Mills,
> Thomas Curtis, and Anne his Wife, were severally imprisoned
> at several Times, for speaking to the Priest and People in the
> Steeple-house at Reading.

Since preaching in itself was not illegal it is clear that these imprisonments were politically motivated and the Quaker witness seen as subversive. There were three prisons at this period in Reading: the town lock-up or 'Compter' by St Laurence, the Borough Prison or 'Bridewell' at Greyfriars, which was a house of correction mainly for women and children, and the County Gaol on Castle Street; at times during the 1660s all three were full of Quakers. With so many prisoners the gaoler complained that 'there was not such another bed in Berkshire.' A Gaol-keeper would charge prisoners for food, drink and bedding; it was often up to prisoners' families to keep and supply them if the gaoler refused this, although depending on their trade the prisoners might have their tools with them and work. We know of Quakers producing silk-laces and shoemaker's pegs while imprisoned in Reading Gaol.

The 'steeple-house' comment is a dismissive Quaker way of referring to the parish church buildings, since the Church is properly the people who meet there, not the building; interrupting the service to question the priest and to preach in his place was standard Quaker practice and women would do this as well as men, to the priests' dismay. In a rigidly hierarchical and class-based society they declared that all men and women were children of God and objected to doffing their hats to their social superiors. As all should always speak the truth, so Quakers refused to swear oaths, like the oath of loyalty compulsory to take any civic office. This was easily backed up with scripture (Matthew 5:34–37, James 5:12) but put them into violent collision with the authorities. Such appeals to Biblical authority aimed to restore the Church to the form it had had in the time of the Apostles, and thus complete the work of the Reformation.

> … and there was never no Priesthood that took Tithes who
> was made by the Law of God, but what was in the time of the
> Law, in the time of the War, which Law Christ ends, and takes
> away the occasion of the War; this Priesthood which takes
> Tithes now, made by Colledges of men, they are neither made
> by the Law nor Ministers of the Gospel, but by the inventions
> of men; So we in the power of the Lord God deny them.
> — from the Berkshire women's petition to abolish tithes, 1659

In this year Thomas Curtis was made militia commissioner for the county of Berkshire and soon afterwards George Fox, who had collapsed into depression following a period of overwork and imprisonment, came to stay with the Curtises in Reading to recover. Quakers were swimming hard against the tide. Restoration of the monarchy in 1660 brought a renewed censorship of the press, and a series of Acts of Parliament attempted to force people back into uniformity with the Church of England. It was, however, the Restoration that turned Quakers toward pacifism; it had not been notable among them before. Many Quakers had in fact been associated with the New Model Army; Thomas Curtis had been a captain in it, or even Royalists like his wife Ann (this spelling of her name is more usual than 'Anne'). In the panics of 1659–60 that preceded the invitation to Charles to take the throne it had been rumoured that General Lambert was arming the Quakers to start a rebellion; a rumour that could have seemed credible in 1659 was barely so two years later.

The Quaker Act of 1662 specified penalties if Friends assembled 'to the number of five', and ordered transportation to the King's plantations abroad for being caught three times at a meeting (hence the long history of Quaker meetings in Barbados); it was one of a series of Acts of Parliament aimed at suppressing dissent. Local magistrates would send out men to find unauthorised religious meetings and to arrest all who were taking part. Reading was already a strong centre for all kinds of independent nonconformity, there being large Baptist and Presbyterian congregations too. The fact that the Quakers refused to hide or to recant once arrested seemed reckless to many but in fact helped them to convert other prisoners once in gaol. Reading Quakers suffered a disproportionate amount of harassment from the authorities, due in large part to the animosity of one man, Justice of the Peace William Armorer, who was particularly zealous in his attempt to stamp out religious dissent.

'On the 8th Day of the 2nd Month called April, 1662' [New Year's Day was 25 March, Lady Day; the year didn't start in January until 1752] Thomas Curtis, George Lamboll and ten others were sent to Reading prison for not attending Church. This was not even strictly illegal; it should have been the remit of the Church courts which had not yet been properly re-established. But thus began a furious period of persecution lasting the next four or five years. After arresting forty-seven Reading Friends on one occasion, the Mayor ordered that the women be left behind, 'there being so many, it may be the Burden was too heavy... to bear, so they were dropped and taken no Notice of...'

On another raid William Armorer cried out ,

> A Devil on you, I could find in my Heart to lay you over the Pate
> with my Cane.

Quaker John Boult replied calmly,

> Thou oughtest to keep the Peace, and I hope thou wilt not
> break it; didst thou ever read that Christ or any of his Apostles
> did persecute?

Armorer answered mockingly,

> Did none? Christ's Flock is but a little Flock, and there is but
> a few of you, but I will make you fewer, I will hunt you out and
> send you to Prison.

Boult answered him,

> That's the weakest thing that thou canst do, if thou canst
> convince me of any thing that is evil, I will hear thee, and
> let the Prisons alone.

Boult was a London shoemaker; it is possible that he may have travelled to Reading to support the cause. By mid-1664 most of the adult male members of Reading Meeting were behind bars and the Justices started on the women. One of the younger women, Anne Harrison, stood up to them, asking,

> Thou hast got our house already that we built, and hast taken
> away our Means, and wouldst thou have me pay more Money,
> when I have broke no Law? We were but four above the Age
> of sixteen Years, but the Act says it must be above four.

By November of that year the authorities began to assault, beat and threaten the children who were keeping the Meetings (and possibly their parents' businesses too) in their absence. We find records of three children being fined twelve pence each for not attending church when they were taken at a Meeting, and ending up in Greyfriars for several months since they were, of course, unable to pay. Several times during the winter months of 1664 Armorer and his men came in 'great fury', and finding only a few children in the Meeting House, pulled them out into the street, beating them 'till some of them have been black in the face'. Armorer sealed their Meeting House with bars and padlocks; the children continued to gather outside. Again they were beaten and despite the winter weather he ordered his constables to throw cold water over them.

The fury of the authorities at this point lost them much sympathy in the town. In January 1665 a group of Quakers were cleared by the jury (technically they were guilty) when it became clear that Armorer had lied in his indictment against them. This only made him angrier.

At the Sessions in January 1666 Mary Winter and Judith Smith were 'convicted of Meeting the third Time and received Sentence ... to be banished to Barbadoes'. This sentence was not actually carried out (in some cases ship owners refused to take prisoners of conscience to the King's colonies) and both women were eventually released from Reading Gaol six years later. More than two hundred Quakers around the country were sentenced to banishment in this way, although in only about a tenth of the cases were they actually transported. The punishment was not used against members of any other church.

Joseph Coale or Cole had been present as a teenager at Hallhead and Salthouse's early meetings in Reading and he soon became an itinerant preacher himself. He published a number of tracts while in prison in Reading and died there in 1670. He wrote:

Neither prison-walls and locks, nor the cruelty of man can
obstruct the issues of the Lord's love, nor the manifestation
of his presence.

The noted Quaker letter-writer Isaac Penington was a friend of the Curtises and was arrested by Armorer whilst visiting them in Reading Gaol in 1670. He was proffered the oath of allegiance and, refusing it, was imprisoned himself.

In the earliest days Friends had had no buildings specifically for meetings but gathered in their own houses or barns. In Reading we know that they took place in the Curtises' large house in 'the Sun backside', behind Sun Lane from 1655. In the year 1671 they built on what was probably the Curtises' land in Back Lane a

Wedding in prison

purpose-built Meeting House, probably of two storeys with two rooms, one above the other. Sun Lane and Back Lane were two streets running parallel to where King Street is now. The Reading Quakers' business meetings were at times arranged in prison, since that was where most of the adults were, and Reading Friends William Yeet and Hannah Wrenn were married behind bars in 1671.

When England and France joined in war against Holland in 1672 the suppression of religious dissent at home dropped from political priorities, and the King issued a Declaration of Indulgence that freed Quakers all across the country from gaol – over seventy were released in Berkshire alone but several had died in prison. This Indulgence did not apply to those imprisoned for withholding church tithes however, as they came under ecclesiastical jurisdiction. Two things seem clear though. One is that as well as suppressing dissent the prosecutors had a financial motive; to seize goods and possessions. Sometimes informers would go to the magistrates hoping for a small cash reward, but the Crown or local authorities stood to gain a lot. In one year (1679) a substantial Quaker farmer, Michael Reynolds at Farringdon in north Berkshire, was 'despoil'd of Cattle, Barley, and Beans for Tythes to the value of more than ninety seven Pounds' – an enormous sum. Leonard Coale in Reading had had goods of a similar value confiscated in 1658. Secondly, the courts were playing a trick. Since it was well-known that Quakers would not swear (there is no double-standard for truth; a yes is a yes, and anyway Jesus had forbidden it) they could be brought up for any offence at all; once in court they could be challenged to take the Oath of Allegiance to the Crown – a refusal to do so would be taken as evidence of treachery, at which point the person's goods could become forfeit to the Crown.

A second period of persecution followed a decade later during the instability and plots of the early 1680s. A petition to the new King James II shows that there were thirty-seven Quaker prisoners in Berkshire (almost 1500 across the country), many of whom now obtained pardons from the King. Even after the Toleration Act of 1689/90 Friends were not entirely secure. This new Toleration was careful to exclude both Catholics and any who questioned the Trinity; a major issue for free-thinking Quakers. All kinds of Dissenters remained on the alert for a reversal of fortune and renewed repression; Tory mobs rioted around the country against them in 1710 and 1715. But the movement was well-rooted. 'Persons of substance in the parish [St Giles in Reading] are few and thin and there's abundance of Quakers there who will not pay anything to the church rates' moaned one poor clerk in 1724; Quakers were still having their possessions impounded for non-payment of these rates decades later. Religious conviction carried a quantifiable cost. In 1721 a Yorkshireman, Luke Cock, recalled that as he struggled with the testimony against paying church tithes his wife railed against him, 'We'se all be ruined: what is thee ganging stark mad to follow t'silly Quakers?' Presently, however, she came round to his state of thinking: "Well,' says she, 'now follow thy Guide, let come what will."

What are Quaker business meetings?

Since the earliest days Quakers have held business meetings that make collective decisions on a range of matters, from managing financial resources to action in the community. They are a type of Meeting for Worship in which Friends discern together how best to proceed; anyone who is part of the Meeting may attend and contribute. Since Quakers have no clergy or paid administrators these meetings are a vital part of running their affairs. Decisions are not made by vote, but by coming together in unity; the aim is collective decision, not majority overrule. In this sense it's not democratic. When agreeing, Friends may often say 'I hope so' (faith) rather than 'yes' (certainty).

II. A split in Reading Meeting

> ❝ God made no difference, but gave his good Spirit, as it
> pleased him, both to Man and Woman... ❞
> — Margaret Fell, 'Women's Speaking Justified', 1666

For about forty years Reading Quaker Meeting split into two factions.

Among Friends, women were ostensibly held to be equal with men. Early Court recorders, annoyingly, did not share this attitude and often label women as just 'ux.' ie, 'the wife of' somebody. Equality caused much contention, particularly over the institution of women's meetings for their business; distribution of money to the poor, placing young women as servants, etc. Few at this point questioned that women and men would have different businesses to manage and that men would deal with property. Equality of the sexes was an exceptionally radical idea four centuries ago and it is fair to say that it was applied unevenly; nevertheless the principle was inspirational. There seems little point in carping that their vision would not meet modern definitions of equality. In every single Friends Meeting House where you can still see separate women's and men's meeting rooms the women's room is smaller (although it is noticeable that in a hefty proportion of those with only one heater for the building, the women got the heating).

It was during the period when many of the men were imprisoned, and in the aftermath of the Great Plague in London of 1665, that separate women's business meetings began:

> because the Men ... found that this Burden grew too heavy for
> them, they offer'd Part of this Service and Care to the most
> grave and solid Women of their Church.

In Reading, Thomas and Ann Curtis (having suffered decades of fines and hardship for the sake of the Meeting they may well have felt some sense of ownership of it) objected to the changes that included these separate women's business meetings. This put them at odds with their old friend George Fox, who was now attempting to tame the wilder elements of early free-thinking Quakers into a more disciplined movement; another new requirement was that Friends wishing to publish should offer their work for scrutiny first. Those who objected felt that Fox was setting himself up as a sole leader, and they framed their concerns as defending belief in the authority of the light within over formal structures; it is notable though that one sticking point was that couples wishing to marry were now asked to submit a request to both men's and women's business meetings for approval.

Did not women already have 'more power than ability to make use of it?', the Separatists asked; this would keep them from their 'household duties'. These arguments were echoed elsewhere in the country and became more intense following a disagreement over the publication of a book by a dissenting Bristol Friend who was supported by Benjamin Coale in Reading. The Separatists took issue with the 'groaning singing or sounding' that often accompanied vocal ministry at this time; a hostile and exaggerated account of Quakers from 1698 describes

> How generally were their Meetings either silent, or taken up with the sudden, and violent irruptions of dismal howling and horrible roarings.

In Reading there was a sharp divide too over whether to meet in secret or to be open, with the more discreet party arguing that those prepared to face public hardship and fines were richer in the first place; the Meeting 'fell into jangling and were disorderly' and eventually split. Differences between the parties became so heated that in 1684 the Curtises locked the Meeting House doors against those who supported the women's meetings (the 'orthodox' party) and eventually bricked up the entrance. No one met there for nine years.

It is astonishing that this bitter split should have persisted in the midst of persecution from the state. The two groups were still meeting for worship together but now had separate business meetings, sometimes in the same room with their backs to each other. Modern descriptions of the episode can show it as an issue over women's space but this is not how it was discussed then and it is worth remembering that women could be part of the main business meeting in the Separatists' plan. Given all this it is a shame that we hear so little of the women's voices throughout it. What is more, the children who had kept the Meeting twenty years earlier would have been adults now and should have had something to say about it, but the prominent voices on both sides were mostly older men. Marriages became a particular site of contention, with both sides complaining that the other was not following due process. In time the Separatist Meeting became entirely dominated by Thomas Curtis as though he were its preacher, and it declined in numbers. The orthodox Meeting in 1692 rented a house from Elizabeth Bryant; the licence describes it as being 'in the Court or backside behind a Messuage or Tenement on the East side of London Street.' This was Sims Court, part of the building now occupied by Reading International Solidarity Centre (RISC).

'Remember my love to all as though I named them'
– from a letter written by George Fox to the Curtises in Reading Gaol

III. William Penn (1644–1714)

A good end cannot sanctify evil means; nor must we ever do evil, that good may come of it… We are too ready to retaliate, rather than forgive, or gain by love and information. And yet we could hurt no man that we believe loves us. Let us then try what Love will do: for if men did once see we love them, we should soon find they would not harm us. Force may subdue, but Love gains: and he that forgives first, wins the laurel.
— William Penn, 1693

The noted Quaker leader and statesman Wiliam Penn is strongly linked to Reading Meeting. He had gone up to Oxford in the momentous year of 1660; a good-looking and popular boy but his rejection of the formalist theology of the day soon caused him problems. 'I never had any religion other than what I felt,' he would write later, and further 'I never addicted myself to school learning to understand religion by but always, even to their faces, rejected and disputed against it.' He was sent down from Oxford for his nonconformity after just a year but was also something of a gallant, at least enough to inspire a twinge of jealousy in Samuel Pepys when he came home one day in 1664 to find the fashionably dressed Penn there talking to his wife.

Pepys probably need not have worried; Penn was already leaning towards the Quakers and in 1667 at a meeting in Ireland he was convinced. Thus began a long career in which Penn was imprisoned often (to the dismay of his father, an admiral, also William Penn) and released often but never ceased to write and worship how he would. He campaigned tirelessly for religious toleration, not just for Quakers but for all the sects even including the often-feared Catholics.

In an important London trial (Bushel's case in 1670) a jury was fined and imprisoned by the judge for acquitting Penn and another Quaker of unlawful assembly but eventually exonerated, confirming the important principle of the jury's independence.

A young William Penn

In settlement of a large debt owed by the Crown to Penn's father, William was granted in 1681 a huge tract of land in America to the west of the Delaware. This was to become Pennsylvania, his ideal community, where liberty of conscience was foremost. Tithes were outlawed and the penal code was progressive for its time. Voltaire remarked of Penn's treaty with the Native Americans that it was the only such treaty never sworn to, and the only one never broken. Unfortunately, not all of Penn's ideals were fully assented to by all the colonists.

Returning from his difficult last visit to America in 1701 Penn settled at Ruscombe, near Twyford. The house, 'on a noble large dry gravely green, and clean ways about it', was demolished in 1840 to make way for the Great Western Railway but it was from here that Penn would, when well enough, ride in to Reading on a Sunday to attend the Meeting, and it was to the orthodox Meeting on London Street that he would come. He was beset in his later years by money troubles and a series of strokes robbed him of the power of articulate speech. One thing that may have cheered him was that the two Quaker factions, both desiring new premises, managed to put aside their differences and reunite in 1715, moving to the present site in Church Street. William Penn died in 1718 and was buried at Jordans Meeting House in Buckinghamshire.

Eliza Langley, who in the 1880s took over Lovejoy's Circulating Library on the London Street Meeting House site (now RISC) and who is buried at Church Street burial ground, commissioned a plaque to William Penn's memory for the building. In 1973 it was rescued from a skip and eventually donated to Reading Museum where it is now on display.

IV. The Church Street Meeting House

Quaker meeting houses do not display a cross nor indeed any visual imagery. The aim of the architecture is to enable quiet listening and peaceful concentration with no distractions. There is no altar, pulpit or organ since there is no communion, preacher or liturgy. It is not true however that there are no sacraments or ministry; it is more that everything is sacramental and anyone can be a minister. Any building could if need be house a meeting; it just needs a roof and seats.

The first Meeting House on the present site in Church Street was built in 1715. It occupied about the same footage as the current building and comprised one large room for worship and two smaller rooms at the western end which were used for the separate men's and women's business meetings. It would have been approached from Church Street though a narrow covered alleyway set between two cottages, opening onto a yard.

In 1835 it was pulled down and the present fine Meeting House of red brick laid in Flemish bond with a slate roof was constructed in its place. The meeting room was heated by four stoves (the alcove for one of them remains) and a covered lobby outside the main south door had fireplaces and men's and women's rooms to right and left. Folk House (next door) contained the Institute Room, kitchen, library and caretaker's accommodation.

Over the course of the later twentieth century, all British Quaker meetings moved from rowed benches to square, polygonal or circular seating arrangements so that the members of the meetings now face each other. At the centre there may be a table with a vase of flowers, but the seating aims to embody a sense of equality among the members of the meeting and acknowledge that ministry may come from anyone, young or old, new to the meeting or long familiar.

If you stand in the centre of the Meeting House now you notice at once how airy it is and well-lit, with huge sash windows reaching

Aerial photo, *c.* 1910

almost up to the ceiling. On a drowsy summer morning the whole room floods with light. On a stormy winter day rain rattles against the high windows but the feeling of the room may be the same. If you look straight above your head, you will see a division in the ceiling; this originally held a wooden partition screen that could be lowered to divide this large room into two for business meetings. This separation of women's and men's business ended in 1896; in a sense you could say that the separatist party of Thomas and

Left to right: Mary Plimsoll, Elizabeth Adley, Anne Simpson, Janet Simpson, Margaret Seaby, Barbara Seaby in 1964, dressed up as the children of Reading Meeting in 1664.

Ann Curtis had won, two hundred years later, as women regained an equal voice in all business matters.

At the west end there is a massive doorway; this seems to have been the original entrance to the Meeting House. It might just have been a coffin door for access to the garden, but if so it seems odd that it should be so tall. You would likely have come in here to find rows of wooden pews all facing the raised elders' bench. Families would originally have split as they walked in, with women and younger children moving to sit on the left and men on the right. There are a few of the wooden pews still in the meeting room, dating back to the nineteenth century. The very first Meeting House here would also have had wooden seating, but these would probably have been plain benches with no backs to them. At the east end you will see the raised bench (or stand) that was reserved for the recognised and travelling ministers, and later the elders. The huge sweeping curve of the wall behind helps to magnify sound so that someone standing here can speak quietly and yet be heard clearly across the room. Elders still sat up on this raised platform in the 1950s but descended to the same level as everyone else soon after.

The lobby buildings were demolished in the 1960s to make way for the present rooms and Folk House next door was sold; it was used as a paint store and then turned into flats. The meeting rooms were substantially added to in 1994. There is a children's room but children are welcomed into the main Meeting House to take part for the first fifteen minutes of the Meeting. Children are often stated to be the future of the Meeting, but they are important parts of the present too.

V. The burial ground and garden

The first Quaker burial ground in Reading was by the London Road, about where the end of Boult Street now is, off Watlington Street. The lease of the plot there had been bought by Thomas Curtis in 1660; it soon needed to be enlarged and adjoining ground was bought, along with an order to dig deeper graves. In 1678 the surrounding wall had broken down and there was a problem with the intrusion of pigs. A member of the Meeting was appointed to dig the graves: in the early days this Friend, usually someone in need of financial support, would be allowed to live in the cottage beside the burial ground. His charges were regulated by the meeting and were set at twelve pence in 1681 when the cost of a funeral is given as ten shillings, although this was not intended 'to Limmitt any friend or friendly people from giving more as they see meet'. Quaker burials consisted solely of a meeting for worship at the graveside where ministry could be offered by anyone present and there were at that time no grave markers. Outward displays of mourning such as decorating the coffin or wearing black hats or arm-bands were disapproved of.

The present burial ground was established in 1715 along with the building of the new Meeting House. In 1833 when Sidmouth Street was laid out the original burial ground was finally closed and in the course of the work

> remains consisting of five hundred and fourteen sculls
> and many other bones were carefully collected and placed
> in four large shells and reinterred in the burial ground
> in Church St Reading.

It was only a few years after the new Meeting House was built, about 1850, that gravestones were allowed in Quaker burial grounds, although some were installed after that date retro-spectively. Initially these were square and level with the ground, but upright stones of a uniform design soon followed. These are meant to be inscribed only with the deceased's name and their dates of birth and death. Once again, rules are often applied unevenly and some wealthy Quaker families around the country did give in

Burial ground

to the vanity of large Victorian-style monuments. In Reading you will see that the markers are generally quite even. They are placed at the foot of the grave and the body is buried behind; they are footstones rather than headstones.

The magnificent fastigiate oak at the centre of the burial ground was planted in 1937 by Rosemary Wallis from an acorn from Bad Pyrmont in Lower Saxony, Germany; forty years later she was buried in its shade. The Quäkerhaus at Bad Pyrmont had been

Oak tree

established in the late eighteenth century and re-established in 1932. During the Second World War it was requisitioned by the Hitler Youth and damaged but was later restored and is still open today. Given the date of the tree and the political tensions of that time the tree was presumably a friendship gesture.

Quaker dress

Early Quakers wore much the same clothes as their contemporaries, but in an age that favoured displays of wealth and status they tended to simple clothes where possible. When King Charles II asked William Penn whether their religious beliefs really differed, Penn replied that the difference was 'the same as between thy hat and mine: mine has no ornaments'. Simplicity in clothing was intended as an outward sign of inner conviction. For some Friends, no change in dress was required: George Fox wore the apron and breeches of a shoemaker long after he had left off the trade. However in Reading it was noted by a contemporary that the Curtises had

> formerly lived very high, and very rich in apparel, but are stripped of all: he hath ripped off his gold buttons, and his wife hath stripped off all her jewels and rich attire.

Adopting Quaker dress brought those in a privileged position like Penn into often fierce conflict with their parents. At court they wore simple styles in good quality fabrics, while poorer Friends wore homespun. By the end of the seventeenth century, conformity in dress had become prevalent and was more enforced within the Society. In 1698 Margaret Fell, then in her eighties, felt that the testimony of simplicity was degenerating into a preoccupation with the way that Friends dressed, the colours they wore, and the furniture used in their houses:

> It's a dangerous thing to lead young Friends much into the observation of outward things which may easily be done. For they can soon get into an outward garb, to be all alike outwardly. But this will not make them into true Christians: it's the spirit that gives life.

In the following century Friends' ways of life were restricted by Overseers, who imposed standards of dress and behaviour as well as giving pastoral support. Quaker clothes and manners became rather codified, retaining older styles both in dress and speech, such as using the archaic forms 'thee' and 'thou'. Quakers were slow to adopt new fashions on principle because fashion was 'vanity', and because they felt that clothes should be durable, worn for many years and handed down. We do know of exceptions, such as Elizabeth Fry who was born into the prosperous Gurney family, and as a young woman wore fashionable clothes like purple boots with red linings. There was some discontent among 'Plain Friends' about the 'Gay Friends' like this; women who wore jewellery and men who wore wigs. However, we can imagine that Reading Friends at the first Church Street meeting house in the 1700s would have looked a little different from Reading folk in general: the men in broad brimmed hats, the women in simple grey or brown dresses, white aprons and bonnets, with shawls or cloaks. Conscience was important: in America John Woolman was an early campaigner against slavery and always wore undyed cloth since the dyeing industry there used enslaved labour.

From around 1830 fashionable men began wearing long trousers and top hats became the norm. Quakers were slow to adopt these new-fangled 'pantaloons' and in this provincial town, male Friends probably still wore breeches and hose for many years. However, after the flamboyance of the preceding centuries, 'normal' clothing for men steadily became more sombre and business-like, which made 'simplicity' easier for Quaker men. Portraits of prominent Quaker businessmen like Huntley, Palmer and Waterhouse all show them wearing the same garb as other professionals.

In 1860 Britain Yearly Meeting gave up the requirement to dress plainly and there was a gradual transition to styles indistinguishable from the general population by the turn of the twentieth century.

VI. Prosperity and umbrellas

Whilst the meeting's story for its first fifty years had been stormy and turbulent, the next century was anything but. It was a time of consolidation and for some, increasing quietism. Freedom from persecution seems to have prompted a collective sigh of relief, but it came at the expense of some campaigning passion. It had been hard work too in the later seventeenth century for Fox and Penn (and others) to discipline a movement that had drawn in so many individualists. The formality of having certain Friends now licensed as 'recognised ministers' may have come to silence voices from elsewhere in the Meeting, but 'travelling in the ministry' became a hugely important way for the Society of Friends to maintain contact and unity, and to visit and support isolated Meetings and individuals.

Early Quakers claimed to be performing miracle cures, something of which their more sober and rational descendants were at times heartily embarrassed. Fox compiled a whole book of his own miracles but then suppressed it. In the 1650s Quakers had aimed to reform the whole world; a hundred years later the end of the world did not seem nearly so imminent and long-term survival became the aim.

But against the prevailing image of an isolated and exclusive Society in the eighteenth century we could place travelling minister Thomas Story's account of his visit to Reading in 1722. The Meeting was attended by

> many of the neighbours of all sorts, and among others, several military officers. The Lord gave me a door of utterance, and a considerable entrance also with Friends and people, the Gospel of the Kingdom of Christ being plainly laid open in doctrine to them, and many well affected among them; and one lieutenant afterwards said that he had never been at any of our Meetings before, or at any other with like satisfaction... and that we were a people very much misrepresented and abused...

There was some contention within Reading Meeting over the way that Quaker orthodoxy was at times heavy-handedly enforced. Some members who, through discretion or inability to afford the fines, had paid their Church tithes were formally excluded from membership, upon which Henry Finch (a prosperous linen-draper in the Market Place) complained that that

> our best-disposed friends, may mistake their own Zeal, for the Revelation of unerring wisdom. No Friend should assume that such a favor is *exclusively* bestowed on him.

The issue was very slow to be resolved, and although it does appear that whilst some who were disowned in this way remained attenders and were eventually buried at the Meeting House, others joined the Church of England instead.

In the later 1700s Quakers found a new cause that brought their voice and witness strongly before the world, in the campaign for the Abolition of the Slave Trade. This was a remarkably successful mission, effecting a major social change against fierce opposition from the property-owning classes within only a few decades; probably because it did not confine itself long only to Quakers but drew in by 1787 progressive Church of England evangelicals like Wilberforce and Clarkson, along with important voices from the Methodists, Congregationalists and others.

Although the town of Reading had no great involvement in the slave trade it submitted a petition against slavery in March 1792. Thirty other towns around the country did likewise but it is unusual to notice that Reading's petition, unlike that from Wallingford for instance, was drafted without the support of the town Corporation. This suggests a possibility that some of the town's more substantial merchants and landowners may have held interests in the trade themselves. An abolition motion in Parliament in response to these petitions was spiked at the last moment by having the word 'gradually' inserted. A major, but partial, victory came in 1807; by 1830 more than two thousand petitions had been submitted to Parliament and soon after the Society of Friends raised £1000 by subscription for the Anti-Slavery Society. Slavery was finally outlawed throughout British territories in 1833. The petitions were lost in a fire at Westminster in 1834 and so cannot now be examined, but it seems certain that Reading Friends would have been signatories to these.

The American travelling minister Job Scott, however, was not impressed by the Quakers of Berkshire on his visit in 1793. They

> seemed in general to have very little sense of any thing
> more in religion than the customary formal performances.
> Tell them any thing about divine life in religion, and they
> seem to think one an enthusiast, and perhaps some
> of them would give a smile of ridicule: yet, to do them
> justice, they are pretty generally civil…

John Man's *History & Antiquities of the Borough of Reading* (1816) is sniffy about the local Quakers too. Declaring them to be 'on the decline', he goes on to state that education

> prompts the younger members of this religious society
> to rise superior to early prejudices, and boldly dare to think
> for themselves.

It is possible that those Friends themselves were more inclined to think this a strength of the Meeting rather than its doom.

Quakers from the 1650s had swiftly established a strong presence in rural Berkshire, particularly up on the Downs. A hundred years later some of these meetings had declined, and the disowning of Quakers who 'married out' – ie, outside the Society – was causing membership problems. A survey of 1716–18 found about 900 Quakers in Berkshire, a third of them in Reading. By Victorian times the Quaker faith was very largely urban, mostly in Reading and Newbury, and the Quaker congregations around Uffington and Abingdon had been largely replaced by Methodist ones.

Who were these Quakers and what were they doing? Many early Friends unsurprisingly were involved in agriculture – they were farmers, millers and so on. Many too were involved in Reading's main trades – in the seventeenth century that had been wool and broad-cloth, and then in the eighteenth century as the wool trade declined the malt trade boomed and supported much of the town's growth. But it is not until the turn of the nineteenth century that we have clear and detailed records of the members of the Society.

We find many references to shopkeepers and to grocers and bakers amongst the lists of members. There are still drapers, a weaver and a calico printer too, showing a continuing presence of the cloth trade. The *Reading Mercury* recorded an objection in 1795 to Quakers opening their shops on Fast-Days, 'in contempt of the Royal Proclamation', and on Christmas Day.

One more unusual trade stands out – umbrella makers. There were at least three local Quaker families involved in this business. Thomas Horniman was an umbrella manufacturer in the town in the last years of the eighteenth century. From 1801 to around 1880, first Thomas Whiting, then his wife Mary and finally their daughter, Emma Pollard, ran a business in London Street as umbrella and parasol makers, also selling rugs and moccasin boots. John Tyler, who married one of Thomas Whiting's daughters, carried on a similar business in Broad Street. The 1848 directory describes him as 'wholesale umbrella & stay manufacturer, agent for Cyrus & James Clark's ladies French & English shoes' – this is the Quaker firm Clarks shoes, of Street in Somerset. He employed four men, a boy, and one hundred women. Quakers were still limited by law in their ability to take part in public affairs, so their impact came via industry, architecture and so on.

VII. The Huntleys and the Palmers

Joseph Huntley, schoolmaster and Quaker minister, is noted first as a member of Reading Meeting in 1811 although he had been known to Reading Friends for much longer both as a prominent member of the Quarterly Meeting and because his wife Mary was herself a Reading girl. Joseph had not prospered as a schoolmaster and in 1822, with the help of his son Thomas, who had trained as a baker, he set up a biscuit bakery on London Street (now number 119) which rapidly gained success. Their turnover in 1837 was more than £1500. Joseph retired in 1838 and Thomas took over the business which was to become the famous Huntley & Palmers; the biscuit factory was built in 1846. The involvement of the Huntley family with this firm ended with the death of Thomas in 1857.

Joseph Huntley junior, one of Joseph's sons, was apprenticed as an ironmonger. He set up business in Reading in 1832 in London Street, opposite his father's bakery, manufacturing stoves and grates and other items. Soon he began manufacturing tin-lined boxes for the biscuit-baking business, a line which became a mainstay of the firm. With the addition of other Quaker partners, James Boorne and Samuel Beaven Stevens, the business expanded, taking on more premises off London Street. With almost a thousand employees they formed a sick club, a burial club and even their own fire brigade. A large area between the Meeting House and Crown Street was taken over by the Huntley, Boorne and Stevens biscuit-tin factory until the 1960s.

George Palmer, who had joined up with Joseph Huntley in 1841, was a Quaker businessman from Somerset, and related by marriage to the Clark (later Clarks) shoe firm. Their firm became the biggest manufacturer of biscuits in the world, and George would go on to become Liberal MP for Reading; the statue of him in Palmer Park originally stood in Broad Street. There is a huge collection of Huntley & Palmers decorated tins in Reading Museum. The firm's products were sold in 172 countries around the world; in Joseph Conrad's 1899 novel *Heart of Darkness*, when the hero fears he is lost in the terrifying Congo jungle he is reassured that he is on his quarry's path by the discovery of a Huntley & Palmers biscuit tin, trodden into the forest floor.

The firm aimed to be an enlightened employer, and in the times before National Insurance and the welfare state the firm set up a sick fund that would look after employees (more than 6000 of them at the firm's peak) in times of hardship. Nevertheless the wages they paid were 'as little as the market would bear' and they were keen to recruit wherever they could pay the least, such as the south Wales valleys during periods of unemployment. Ironically for a Quaker George Palmer was a pretty poor listener, especially when staff came asking for higher wages. Perhaps he was rather better as a benefactor than a collaborator.

George's brother William Isaac Palmer was involved with the temperance movement in Reading and set up the Palmer Memorial Hall in West Street. Jean Palmer (wife of George's son Walter) was a close friend of Constance Wilde, who with her husband Oscar visited the Palmers at their house Westfield by the Bath Road, and Jean looked after the Wildes' younger son Vyvyan several times when he was ill; in later life Vyvyan vividly remembered being taken to the factory and given biscuits hot from the oven. This second generation of Reading Palmers, however, left the Society of Friends; politically they switched from Liberalism to Conservatism and ethically from refusing public honours to welcoming them. When Alfred Palmer joined the Church of England in 1905 the Quaker connection with the firm ended.

VIII. The Waterhouse family

Alfred and Mary Waterhouse, originally from Liverpool, moved to Reading in 1859 to take up residence in the newly built Whiteknights House. It had been designed for them by their son, the Gothic Revival architect also called Alfred Waterhouse. Under the influence of Ruskin and following visits to Venice, Waterhouse began to make his mark with a grand, Gothic style – a far cry from Quaker simplicity. Alfred senior was a retired cotton broker and Mary was a Quaker minister.

The younger Alfred Waterhouse (most famous for Manchester Town Hall and London's Natural History Museum) had his practice in London but built his own house, Foxhill, on the Whiteknights estate and later another not far away at Yattendon. He added to Reading's notable Gothic buildings with Reading School (1868–72), the Town Hall (1875), and just around the corner from the Meeting House the current Rising Sun Arts Centre (1877). East Thorpe House was built in 1880 for Alfred Palmer (George's son), and later given to the University; it became St Andrew's Hall of Residence and is now the Museum of English Rural Life. Waterhouse's reputation dipped in the first half of the twentieth century when many such buildings, including some of his masterpieces, were seen as 'Gothic monstrosities' and pulled down, but has rebounded now and his works are widely celebrated and admired. Although he left the Society in the 1870s his wife Elizabeth (1834–1918), herself an accomplished craftswoman and writer, remained a Quaker and her story *The Island of Anarchy* (1887) is a fascinating moral fable advocating a kind of Christian anarchism.

IX. Reading Quakers and education

When no-one outside the Church of England was permitted to take part in civic affairs or stand for public office, the Society of Friends was necessarily somewhat separate from the town, but this began to change in the nineteenth century. In the high Victorian era the levelling spirit had receded some way; decency and reform were the order of the day. Sunday Schools – known as First-Day Schools – were set up. Reading Quakers around the turn of the twentieth century were involved in a vast number of improving social initiatives, typically things like the Anti-Gambling League. The Meeting would also commit to supporting its own members financially where appropriate. A Monthly Meeting Institute was established in 1890, organising lectures and evening debates but attendance may have been patchy; a decade or so later it was complained that 'there are many friends who are rarely if ever seen at our meetings.'

Reading Quakers were deeply involved in the reception and housing of over 200 Belgian refugees in the town in 1914. Prominent among these Friends was the formidable Henry Marriage Wallis (father of Rosemary), a local magistrate and prolific writer with a 'sonorous, booming voice', whose strident right-wing views made him a controversial figure. He supported British involvement in both the Boer and the Great Wars, against the Peace testimony, and had nothing but scorn for conscientious objectors. He vigorously opposed women's suffrage too and was moved to fury when he saw a female member of Reading Meeting – probably Patty Stansfield – campaigning with a sandwich board in Broad Street. Wallis's business partner as corn merchants was William Henry Smith; not the same person as his namesake and contemporary, the founder of W. H. Smith booksellers, but a Reading Quaker involved in founding East Reading Adult School in 1905. This was another outreach enterprise, quite consciously conceived as being from the well-off to those below. It had some successes in its own right although it was noticed that few very people joined the Meeting from it. The Meeting did note concerns around this time about 'our own exclusiveness' and that this might put off the working classes, as

'...it may be that our method of worship does not appeal to them.' In time the Adult School became too dependent on the time and labour of one man (C. E. Stansfield) and it eventually foundered in 1915.

As the last barriers to Quakers taking public office fell in the later nineteenth century, Leighton Park School was founded in south Reading in 1890 (some said as the 'Quaker Eton') with four pupils and large ambitions, specifically to educate boys for the universities. The fluctuations in relationships between the School and Reading Meeting have reflected some ambivalence in Quaker attitudes and changes in general attitudes in society. Some Quakers have felt fee-paying education is socially divisive while others have seen it as a way of preserving something distinctively Quaker. Until 1913 all boys processed twice every Sunday to Church Street, wearing dark suits, top hats and gloves. It was a very different world from today. A girl's school run by the Misses Sharp also attended Reading meeting on Sundays but it is reported that a joint party held with Leighton Park 'was stopped when the Head Girl was discovered holding the hand of a blushing young Leightonian'. The girls were marched home *en masse* to their school on the Bath Road.

Girls were admitted to Leighton Park too from 1975. Nowadays the Thursday morning Meeting for Worship at the school is deeply valued and is at the heart of students' Quaker experience, allowing a period of calm reflection and orientation to people of every faith and none. There is still an emphasis on translating these values into practical action both while still at school and in later employment. Local Quakers are well represented on Leighton Park's board of Governors and, at an annual meeting, the Head and the Chair of Governors have to give an account of the year to an audience of questioning Friends drawn from all over the country.

X. Phoebe Cusden (1887–1981)

Although born into a staunchly Conservative family the young Phoebe Blackall (later Cusden) left the Church of England when she heard the Bishop of Reading recruiting for the First World War; she could not reconcile this with the teachings of Christ. A teenage activist, she had got into early trouble when trying to unionise the Huntley & Palmers factory workers. Always outspoken on women's issues in her hometown, she was elected to Reading town council in 1931 in the wake of full women's suffrage. She became a magistrate in the same year and was a passionate campaigner for the Nursery School Movement.

Although she pointed out that the council's failure to deal with the Housing crisis of the time owed something to it being 'dominated by landlords' she was a pragmatic fixer rather than an idealist, prepared to work with the Tories if the cause was right. She was a dauntless and tireless worker and the list of organisations that she chaired or co-ordinated is exhausting just to read. Her pacifist convictions only grew stronger during the Second World War, putting her at odds sometimes with her Labour Party colleagues, and at the close of hostilities she threw herself at once into relief projects in Germany, collecting food and clothing in Reading, especially children's, to take over. This work brought her praise and support from many and fierce criticism from others. There were quieter friendship gestures going on too: German Prisoners of War still held for some time at the camp at Basildon Park came to Reading Meeting House weekly for tea and cakes. Phoebe was elected Mayor of Reading too and was very soon organising relief work much closer at hand during the devastating Caversham floods of 1947.

Out of the German reconstruction work came perhaps Phoebe Cusden's best-known achievement, the Reading–Düsseldorf link that grew to involve the towns' twinning and a long series of first humanitarian and later cultural exchanges. 'When you have finished saving Europe,' her husband once asked her, 'will you sew a button on my coat?' Unsurprisingly she retorted that were he properly brought up he would have sewed it on himself. Her Internationalist

Phoebe Cusden

perspective embraced work with the Women's Peace Movement and the Women's International League of Peace & Freedom; she played a role in the Campaign for Nuclear Disarmament (CND) and in facilitating the Aldermaston marches and was a strong supporter of the Reading Race Relations Committee. She spoke her mind at all times and made enemies, but even they had to give her some respect. She became an elder of Reading Meeting at the age of 88 and was still campaigning for various causes well into her nineties; her best testimony is probably the number of people's lives that she improved in Reading and elsewhere without most of them ever even knowing her name.

XI. Ted Milligan (1922–2020)

Although his father, uncles and brother were all engineers, the young Edward Milligan was mystified by things mechanical and, following formative experiences in school libraries, decided on a career as a librarian. He had a horror of extravagance but books were an exception. His library took over all the houses in which he lived although he was generous in passing books on to anyone he felt could make better use of them.

Ted's education was interrupted by the Second World War, during which he registered as a conscientious objector and worked with the Friends Relief Service, first in London and then at Killeaton House, County Antrim, a hostel for elderly people evacuated from the bombing of Belfast: this was the beginning of a life-long interest in and attachment to Irish Quakerism. He was the librarian of Friends House Library in London from 1957 to 1985, where his management style was described as democratic but with an unseen layer of diplomacy: mediation was an essential skill for him.

Ted was extraordinarily knowledgeable on many aspects of Quaker history, and it was during the late 1950s that he started on the studies that led to the invaluable collection of research tools which eased work for those who used the Library in the days before the internet – in particular the typescript *Dictionary of Quaker Biography* – and which culminated in his monumental *Quakers in Commerce and Industry 1775–1920,* published in 2007.

Whilst he lived in Reading and was part of the Meeting here Ted also served London Yearly Meeting at different times on at least eleven committees. He was often approached as a good person to speak to about personal problems or problems arising between members of a Quaker Meeting. On occasion it would be about someone who was gay and before society's outlook on these matters began to change. The irony of this was not lost on Ted since he was himself homosexual. It made him very private about himself; it may have given him empathy but it also gave him determination to live independently of what others thought. Sometimes he could feel cut off from and cut himself off from the understanding of others. Yet Ted's most often remarked-upon gift was his talent for friendship and encouragement. In an article he wrote as a young man he spoke of the times 'when the tides of faith seem far out' and of the Friends 'who have brought light to my darkness … because they were sensitive to God's leadings'; he finished with an exhortation to which he himself certainly responded: 'Do we seek to be the channels of God's love and caring? "Caring matters most."'

❝ I don't know that Quakers have ever had a universal creed for exactly what God is. My personal belief is when we say there is 'That of God in every man' we ought to add an extra letter 'o' and say there is 'That of Good in every man.' And there is a corollary to it: 'There is that of the devil in every man'; it is our job in life to try and bring that of God forward ... ❞
— Don Gill, 2014

❝ There is a light which enlightens the soul, or it remains in darkness: Ye were darkness, said the Apostle, but now are ye light in the Lord. Now, no man can become light in the Lord, unless his nature and spirit be renewed, and changed out of darkness into light... O, come, be not wedded to your own ways, nor prejudiced against what God hath taught others; but let things be fairly scanned, that all things may be proved [tested], and that which is good, hold fast; for truth will not lose ground by being tried, but darkness is afraid of the light... ❞
— Isaac Penington, letter written from Reading Gaol, 1671

❝ I have sometimes wondered why I often don't feel the presence of God. Then I remembered the Taizé chant, 'Ubi caritas' which translates as 'Where there is Love, there is God.' ❞
— Ruth Burke, 2014

XII. Ministering at Reading Meeting

Elisabeth Salisbury, 1968

For some weeks before this particular Sunday I had been puzzling over and questioning in my mind various problems connected with my work. It was one of those episodes of spiritual upheaval which most of us go through from time to time when we seem to question our normal certainties, poke around the foundations of our normal life and discover to our alarm that some of them are very shaky. I had been in this highly charged state for several weeks.

On this Sunday morning though, I went quietly to meeting with the family, my recent preoccupations submerged by the business of getting us all dressed and breakfasted and to the meeting house on time. But as the minutes ticked by and I sat in the healing peace, I began to be aware that something inside me was formulating a question which urgently needed to be asked. I say 'something inside me' because it seemed at the same time to be both me and not me. I discovered to my horror that this something was urging me to get up and ask my question. My heart was pounding uncomfortably and I began to shiver (I don't know whether this was obvious to those around me; I was certainly aware of this shivering but shyness prevents one from asking afterwards whether these physical symptoms are visible to others). To start with I resisted this prompting. I looked round the room and noticed several Friends before whom I was reluctant to make a fool of myself. I could not get up and speak in front of them. I would rather die first. The shaking and pounding diminished a little as I decided this. But not for long. Soon it started up again, insistent, not to be denied. This time I told myself 'I'll count twenty and then if no one else has spoken I shall have to.' Again a slight abatement of the symptoms. But to no avail. I counted twenty and then fifty and still no one spoke. Now I sat conscious only of this overpowering force which was pushing me to my feet until finally I had to give in to it.

Afterwards I found it difficult to believe that I had spoken. It was all over so quickly. Had I really stood up in front of all those people and testified? Well, hardly testified, but yes, I had been driven by some inner prompting which, for want of a more precise word, one might well call spirit; and yes, I had quaked, most fearfully, with something which was more than just the fear of making a fool of myself before family and friends.

Quoted from *Quaker Faith & Practice,* 2.58

XIII. What is Reading Meeting now?

We told the story of the twentieth century largely through the lives of two people – Phoebe Cusden and Ted Milligan – both extraordinary characters and of course neither typical of anything. But a Meeting is made up of many individuals. Most people's lives are less busy and less full than theirs but may yet contain some important work or quiet heroism that is unique to them. Reading Meeting is developing and changing now as it always must.

One of the most notable changes this century has been the move towards marriage equality. Quakers are proud to have been the first church in the world to offer fully equal marriage, in 2009. It is worth noting that a Quaker wedding differs in an important way from both a Church wedding and Register Office one. In the first a minister marries the couple and in the second the registrar does it, but in the Meeting House the couple marry each other, and everyone present is witness to that. The principle here is that marriage is God's business, not ours, and we have been delighted to witness same-sex marriages here in recent years.

In the early years two of the things for which Quakers were best known were the refusal to pay 'hat honour' (to take off your hat before a presumed social superior) and the refusal to pay tithes; in the eighteenth century it was the insistence on plain grey clothing. Society has changed so much that none of these has the meaning now that it did then but Friends' opposition to slavery and insistence on inclusion resonate very strongly today. Some find the early history of Quakers a burden and want to define an entirely modern version of the faith; others love the language and the traditions. Some have argued (or assumed) that Quakers should not drink or smoke but we know of tobacconists and brewers among earlier Friends; some say today that you should not speak twice in a Meeting for Worship but that was not uncommon in earlier days. Perhaps not everyone is comfortable with their own lights, and some would rather be told how to feel.

Early Friends were evangelical, preaching and seeking to convert. This impulse declined and emigration to America reduced numbers. For many years most Quakers were those brought up in the

Meeting – in recent years those who have come to the Meeting from outside predominate, from other churches or none. Some people retain a dual membership with another faith group and bring an extra dimension to the meeting that way.

From the late 1950s on, Reading Meeting helped with hosting the Aldermaston marches (these were large popular campaigns against nuclear weapons); Newbury Meeting was more closely involved with the Women's Peace Camp at Greenham Common US Air Base in the 1980s but there were many links and Berkshire Anti-Nuclear Campaign (BANC) had Reading Meeting House as their base. Reading Quaker Joe Sturge was involved in coordinating both this and Cruise Watch (Cruise was the name for the intercontinental nuclear missiles held at Greenham). Lesli Wilson had taken part in both too and joined Reading Meeting in 1987, shortly after being prosecuted for cutting the fence at Burghfield Atomic Weapons

Establishment. Reading Meeting supported BANC with funding but it is fair to say that some older members were uncomfortable with the militancy of some of these actions, such as the Christian CND Ash Wednesday protests that involved painting messages on the Ministry of Defence buildings in Whitehall with charcoal ash (blessed by a bishop, although Quakers don't need that bit). But the way that these campaigns mobilised and engaged an often female-led movement was startling, effective, and has not gone away. In April 2022 environmental activists from Extinction Rebellion closed off several of the major London bridges in protest against the continued use of fossil fuels; at one point Blackfriars Bridge was held by a single person, 76 year-old Lucy Harding, also a member of Reading Meeting.

Courthouse protest

As this book was being written in 2023 a woman who held a placard outside a London court reminding the jury that they had the right to acquit or convict according to their conscience (this was established following one of William Penn's trials, Bushel's Case, 350 years before) was arrested and charged with contempt of court. Lucy Harding and Amanda Griffin (of Wallingford meeting) immediately organised protests against this travesty of law, and other Reading Quakers like Magda Koc, Stephen Mandel and Jo Rado have been involved in the courthouse vigils.

Quakers work without clergy or paid staff, other than the resident warden. Within any Quaker Meeting, people are appointed to take on a variety of roles; Elders (spiritual life), Pastoral Friends (welfare), Premises (buildings) Clerks (administration) Trustees (charitable status), Children's and Young Person's Committee. The unprecedented crisis of 2020 threw all these roles into sharp relief, and how the Meeting coped at that time illustrates its workings well. At first, Friends worshipped only at home but soon Elders had set up online worship. Pastoral Friends kept in touch with most people by phone, especially the most vulnerable. An on-line coffee morning and a weekly online diary allowed Friends to drop in and share news. Business meetings continued online, and the children benefited from online groups. Although everyone missed meeting in person, worshipping online proved to be surprisingly spiritual for some Friends, with a quiet intensity – and the ability to hear all ministry clearly. The Covid-19 Group met regularly, and also developed the technical set-up which allowed 'Blended Meetings' – a mixture of on-line and in-person worship – when the Meeting House eventually re-opened again a year later. Since then the Meeting has been slowly restoring many things which had had to be given up, from Elders shaking hands to flowers on the table and refreshments in the Hall. Some positive changes are here to stay. All kinds of meetings are held online now, avoiding the need to book a room or to travel.

Reading Meeting House itself has for many years been host to other organisations – the Liberal Jewish Congregation and Reading Interfaith Group for example, and Ploughshares and Refugee Support groups. Whilst the Society of Friends as a whole and local meetings too are involved with a sometimes bewilderingly large number of campaigning groups and charities, Reading Mediation Centre for instance, individual members will always follow their own lights as to where and how they invest their time and energy.

In the coming years it may well be that a commitment to sustainability and practical peace-making (conflict resolution, refugee support, etc.) may be our defining features, but it is not for us to say what the Society of the future will be; our place is in the now.

And yet there is a continuity across the centuries. It is hard to imagine the closely intermarried clans of the nineteenth century. We cannot know what was in the minds of those who sat in this building and wrestled with finding the right responses to two World Wars or to a host of other issues, some now forgotten, any more than we can really inhabit the minds of those Friends who met for worship in Reading Gaol in the 1660s to the bafflement of their fellow prisoners (if there was room for any). But we know *how* they came to each crisis. We know that it was in every case through a collective, sustained waiting in silence for the right words, the right approach, to arrive. From the outside pacifism looks like something passive but in the moment it is often the hardest option to take. Equality too is hard-fought-for. Justice is usually achieved – if it is achieved – at the expense of the powerful and we must understand that here in the developed world that might mean ourselves. There is no one right way to be a Quaker, easy answers are not encouraged and the truth – or the right answer – often arrives by an unexpected route. Simply speaking the truth can get you into trouble; in an unjust world so it should, and Quakers will always believe in creating a space for people to maintain those awkward truths.

Acknowledgements

Written by Geoff Sawers, 'Quaker Dress' by Izzy Brimelow.

Illustrations by Izzy Brimelow, except for the photographs on pages 17 and 18 from the collection of Bob and Liz Brown, and 'Peace in the World' by Emer, Jesse, Daisy, Matilda and Thomas.

Sarah Griffin, Vicky Hummell and Chris Skidmore all gave exceptionally valuable thoughts and advice on the early history of the meeting. Elizabeth Salisbury's testimony is quoted from *Quaker Faith & Practice*, 2.58, with thanks. Thanks too to Bob Brown, Ian House, Anne Nolan, Adam Stout, Lesli Wilson and Jill York. Any mistakes remaining can safely be laid at Geoff's door.

Two Rivers Press has been publishing in and about Reading
since 1994. Founded by the artist Peter Hay (1951–2003), the press
continues to delight readers, local and further afield, with its varied list
of individually designed, thought-provoking books.